Taking the Kids

Other books in the *Taking the Kids* series:

Taking the Kids to the Great American Southwest
Taking the Kids to Northern California
Taking the Kids to Sunny Southern California

Taking the Kids

Everything That's Fun to Do and See for Kids—and Parents Too!

Eileen Ogintz

HarperCollins*West*
A Division of HarperCollins*Publishers*

Taking the Kids™ is a trademark of Eileen Ogintz.
Games created by Alice Binsfeld.

FIRST EDITION

Library of Congress Cataloging–in–Publication Data

Ogintz, Eileen.
 Taking the Kids to the Pacific Northwest: Everything That's Fun to Do and See for Kids—and Parents Too! / Eileen Ogintz
 p. cm. – (Taking the Kids)
 ISBN 0-06-258580-0 (pbk. : alk. paper)
 1. Northwest, Pacific—Guidebooks—Juvenile literature.
 2. Children—Travel—Northwest, Pacific—Juvenile literature.
 3. Family recreation—Northwest, Pacific—Guidebooks—Juvenile literature.
 (1. Northwest, Pacific—Guides.)   I. Title.   II. Series.
 F852.3.035 1995   94-34972
 917.9504'43—dc20   CIP
                                                          AC

95 96 97 98 99 RRD(C) 10 9 8 7 6 5 4 3 2 1

To my newest niece, Erica Jill, and my nine other nephews and nieces: Zach, Adam, Chris, Alex, Michael, Kyle, Angela, Allison, and Audrey. May you always love discovering new places.

To Andy, Matt, Reggie, and Melanie. Thanks for making every place we go an adventure.

This book couldn't have been written without the enthusiastic help and support of many people across the Pacific Northwest in the United States and British Columbia—museum staff, national park rangers, tourism officials, and families who live there. All took time from busy schedules to share their expertise and insights.

Special thanks to Oregon's Susan Bladholm and Washington State's Carrie Wilkinson and David Blandford for helping to arrange the logistics. Thanks to the experts at the Oregon Coast, Seattle, and Vancouver aquariums and the Whale Museum on San Juan Island for helping me to understand salmon, orcas, and the other wondrous creatures who live in these waters.

Thanks to Todd Musburger for his advice, Alice Binsfeld for her teacher's perspective, Stephanie Meismer for her fact-checking, and Joann Moschella, Beth Weber, and the rest of the HarperCollins crew for working so hard to make *Taking the Kids* a success.

he kids walked the whole way—2,000 miles from Missouri to
Oregon—alongside their parents' covered wagons. Many of
them didn't have shoes.

There were so many children on the Oregon Trail that it
became known as "The Family Trail." The nearly 350,000 people

who followed the trail in the 1840s marked the largest voluntary migration in U.S. history. Families carried all their possessions in wagons that were much smaller than mini-vans. There wasn't room to bring a lot of toys. When it rained, there was no place to stay dry. When their food ran out, they couldn't go to the supermarket for more. There were no TVs, no tape players, and few books. And when they got sick, there weren't any doctors. They traveled for months.

These pioneers settled the Northwest, establishing farms and opening businesses. They changed the shape of this country forever.

FACT:

Nearly half of Oregon is covered by forest. No wonder the state produces 8 million Christmas trees a year, a quarter of all the Christmas trees in the U.S. It takes at least 7 years for a Christmas tree to grow 6 feet tall.

Although the trip was dangerous and often uncomfortable, it was also a great adventure. You can get the flavor of life on the trail by joining a wagon train journey at the National Historic Oregon Trail Interpretive Center in Baker City.

As the pioneers reached a town called The Dalles, near the end of the trail, they

faced their hardest decision: should they try to raft across the swift-flowing waters of the Columbia River, or risk their broken-down wagons on the treacherous land route around Mount Hood? Either way could spell disaster.

Today, families like yours come from all over the country to the Columbia River Gorge to hike, fish, windsurf, and ski. As you watch windsurfers bobbing in the water of the Columbia River, it's difficult to imagine the hardships that the pioneers endured.

Check out those waterfalls! There are 77 on the Oregon side of the Columbia River Gorge. Multnomah Falls drops 620 feet, making it one of the tallest waterfalls in the country. Hike to the top or skim rocks in the pool at the bottom. Wade up the narrow Oneonta Gorge to see the hanging gardens or stop for a picnic at Horsetail Falls. You can follow the trail up to Pony Tail Falls. You can camp nearby at Eagle Creek or hike the Eagle Creek Trail. Many kids think it's one of the prettiest.

FACT:

Forests in the Northwest are home to the northern spotted owl. Today, people are looking for new ways to use forests that will help the northern spotted owl and other animals to survive. Listen for these owls in the woods. Their high-pitched hoot sounds like a small dog barking.

Ancestors of today's Native American tribes lived and fished along the Columbia River's banks. Later, friends and explorers Meriwether Lewis and William Clark covered this ground in 1803 when President Thomas Jefferson asked them to explore the wilderness west of the Missouri River.

It took more than a year for the expedition to cross the country. They traveled over 3,500 miles from the

Missouri River across the Rockies to the Columbia River and the

FACT:

Oregon-based Nike, Inc., uses recycled gym shoes to help build playgrounds. Nikes were invented to help athletes run faster.

Pacific Ocean. A teenage Native American woman named Sacagawea, who had been kidnapped by another tribe as a child, helped guide the explorers. She was reunited with her family on the way.

Along the way, Lewis and Clark drew maps, naming rivers and mountain passes. Most important, their eyewitness accounts inspired the families who would travel the Oregon Trail and settle the West. Visit the Lewis and Clark Interpretive Center at the mouth of the Columbia River, on the Washington side, in Fort Canby State Park to find out more about their expedition.

Nowadays, families travel parts of the Lewis and Clark route on their way to Mount Hood for hiking or cross-country skiing. At 11,235 feet high, Mount Hood is the tallest mountain in Oregon.

Head for the Mount Hood Skibowl. See the snowboarders? They're at it even in July. Mount Hood is the only place for year-round skiing in North America. Take the skychair all the way up and ride a mountain bike down (you can rent one at the top). There's a half-mile double Alpine Slide, too. You can follow the Oregon Trail as you cross-country ski or hike here. Look for the rope  burns on the trees where the pioneers lowered their wagons down these steep slopes.

The pioneers never would have imagined a city like Portland, only 50 miles away. Portland was also founded by adventurers. Two of them beached their canoe by the side of the Willamette

River. They named the place by flipping a penny; Portland is a city in the winner's home state of Maine. (The loser would have named it Boston.)

Today, Portland is a thriving city with plenty of activities for kids. Start at the Oregon Museum of Science and Industry (OMSI, as the locals call it). Built along the banks of the Willamette River, it's got 6 huge exhibit areas packed with hundreds of hands-on science projects. Touch a tornado or tour the submarine USS *Brueback.* Send a message to outer space or build a bridge. Try out

CATCH THE WIND

Ask a windsurfer where's the best place to go for their sport, and you'll most likely be told that it's the Columbia River, which has winds that blow from 5 to 35 miles per hour.

Windsurfing didn't become popular until the 1980s, but today it's the fastest growing water sport in the U.S. One and a half million people enjoy it every year. Now that equipment for children is available, more and more kids are trying. Imagine learning to windsurf in gym class. Some local kids do.

All you have to do is balance on the board, hang on to the sail, and catch the wind. Ready to try?

new computer games. There's enough to keep you busy for days.

Stop by Pioneer Square. Visit Powell's City of Books. People say it's the biggest bookstore in the entire country, with more than a million books, including a roomful just for kids.

If you're ready for some outdoor fun, head across town to Washington Park and the zoo. But first stop in at the World Forestry Center (it's across the parking lot) to learn about the trees of the Northwest. There's even a giant talking tree.

Then work your way around the world at the zoo. Start with Africa: visit monkeys in the rain forest and zebras on the savanna. Go to the Alaskan tundra to check out bears and see beavers at the Cascade Exhibit.

Don't miss the elephants. This zoo is famous for breeding them.

Portland is famous for its roses, too. There are more than 500 varieties in the Rose Test Gardens! Every year, more than 10,000 kids decorate their bikes, wagons, and pets for the Rose Festival Junior Parade, the country's biggest children's parade.

Ready, set, march!

KIDS! TELL YOUR PARENTS:

Skiing can be a great family sport, but only if everyone wants to try. No one should be forced to ski if they're not ready. Your parents may want to invest in some lessons so everyone in the family can get comfortable before starting. Experts say it's really hard for parents to teach their own kids.

Whether you're going downhill or cross-country skiing, make sure everyone has the appropriate clothing: weatherproof pants, gloves, and jackets; heavy socks; wool hats and sweaters. There's nothing like soggy mittens or wet socks to ruin a day on the slopes. And don't forget to put on sunscreen.

For information about Mount Hood, call the Mount Hood Visitors Center at 503-622-4822. Call the Columbia River Gorge Visitors Association and the Columbia River Gorge National Scenic Area at 503-386-2333. For windsurfing information, call the U.S. Windsurfing Association at 503-386-8708. In the town of Hood River, Big Winds specializes in teaching kids how to windsurf; call 503-386-6086.

Call the National Historic Oregon Trail Interpretive Center at 503-523-1843 and the Portland Visitors Association at 800-962-3700.

Oregon Trail Make-a-Word

Match a group of letters from the left column with a group of letters in the right column to form a word or a name.

MISS	UMBIA
ORE	CITY
COL	VER
RI	EERS
DAL	IL
PION	ON
WAG	GON
MOUNT	LES
BAKER	OURI
TRA	HOOD

_____

_____

_____

_____

_____

_____

_____

_____

_____

_____

(Answers are on page 108)

18

rab those buckets and shovels, and a big round plastic sled, too. Then head for the sand.

We're talking giant hills of sand, hundreds of feet high. There are more than 40 miles of dunes to explore at the Oregon Dunes National Recreation Area near Florence, as well as 400 miles of coast, most of it fronted by beach. The entire Oregon coast is open to the public. Enjoy it wherever you and your family decide to stop.

Build huge sand castles, race your sister or brother up the beach, write your name in giant sand letters, and toss a ball. Hunt for driftwood, pieces of wood that have been shaped by waves rushing over them and washed ashore. Or explore tide pools—rocky areas along the beach that are filled with seawater and

BEACH SMARTS

For a trouble-free day at the beach:

- **Always wear sunscreen and a hat. Take a break in the shade every 90 minutes or so. And drink plenty of water.**

- **Never swim alone. When exploring the beach, always keep one eye on the sea. Don't be surprised by strong currents and big waves.**

- **Never play on a log near the water. If the waves push it, you can be hurt.**

- **If you see someone in trouble, run and yell for help. Don't try to rescue that person yourself.**

- **Pick up and discard litter.**

- **Be prepared for cool days. Even though you'll be at the beach, you should bring along some warm clothes, including a jacket.**

teeming with sea life. Watch for the many different seabirds that are to be found along the Oregon coastline—among them, pelicans, cormorants, gulls, and egrets.

Head to Cannon Beach to see the gigantic Haystack Rock. Many people try to climb it.

Have you ever made a sand angel? Lie on your back and move your arms back and forth. When you get up, you'll have left an angel just your size in the sand.

Oregon sand is a combination of crushed shells and tiny grains of rock that have been here for thousands of years. Some of the dunes are more than 400 feet high. The sand in the dunes "dances" with the wind, moving as much as 12 feet inland every year. You can ride down the dunes on a sled—the inexpensive round plastic kind is especially slippery if you wax the bottom. Some people explore the dunes in a

N

Lincoln City
Newport
Yaquina Bay
Florence
Honeyman State park

Oregon Dune Nat. Recreational Area

Oregon

CHOPPER!

dune buggy. The ride is bumpier than a roller coaster!

Many families like to camp or picnic in the dunes. Several freshwater streams and lakes are nearby. The lake at Honeyman State Park, just south of the town of Florence, is fun to visit because you can slide down the sand straight into the water! But watch out for quicksand in low, wet areas. It's not dangerous, but you could get stuck.

While you're on the coast, stop and see a lighthouse. Lighthouses were built to warn ships at sea that they are dangerously close to shore. There are 10 lighthouses along the Oregon coast. The Heceta Lighthouse, north of Florence, is the most photographed lighthouse in the country, so be sure to bring your camera!

TIDE POOLS

Tide pools are rocky pockets by the seashore that hold water when the tide goes out. Some are large, and others are very small. They're home to a wide assortment of sea life, including anemones, sponges, sea slugs, mussels, crabs, starfish, and sea urchins. The best time to explore is during low tide. (Pick up a local tide table to find out tide times.) Try Cape Peretua, Otter Rock, or Devil's Punch Bowl.

Step carefully—the ground is slippery! And remember that life clings to almost every surface here. The creatures in tide pools are fragile. If you handle any of them, put them back exactly where you found them. Don't take anything home. An empty shell can provide a home for another animal in the future.

And always keep one eye on the sea. Waves can sneak up on you.

You'll also want to visit the Sea Lion Caves, just a mile south of the Heceta Lighthouse. An elevator takes you down 208 feet to a cave that is home to some 200 Stellar sea lions. You will see dozens of them stretched out on the rocks. Some sea lions weigh up to a ton. Do you hear them all barking?

This is also a good place to be on the lookout for gray whales, especially between the months of December and April. That is when they travel south from Alaska to the warm waters of

Mexico's Baja Peninsula, where they have their babies, and then head north again.

The whales manage to make the 5,000-mile trip twice a year, traveling in small groups and staying fairly close to shore. It's the longest distance any mammal migrates. They surface every few minutes to breathe. Look for the "blow"—that's the cloud of air and water the whale spews out! A blow can be as high as 15 feet and happen as often as every 30–50 seconds. To see them, go early in the morning to the coastal headlands that jut out into the ocean. Overcast days are good bets because there is little glare off the water.

If you are lucky, you'll see the whales jump out of the water and fall back, making a big splash. This is called "breaching." Don't forget to bring your binoculars.

Just north of the Sea Lion Caves in Newport, the Oregon Coast Aquarium is a great place to find out more about all of the sea life you're finding. In case you've missed

FACT:

You have Oregon to thank for the peppermint flavor in your toothpaste and Christmas candy canes. Oregon produces more peppermint than any other state.

anything, the aquarium has designed four acres outdoors to represent coastal life, complete with tide pools, sea caves, and the animals that live there. You can watch sea lions, harbor seals, and fuzzy sea otters. See the otters blow air into their fur? They do that to keep warm and to stay afloat, puffing up their fur like a down vest.

While you are at the aquarium, walk through the Seabird Aviary to see such unusual birds as tufted puffins (they dress up for their mating games, growing long tufts of yellow feathers) and rhinoceros auklets. Then head inside to see jellyfish, salmon, and more. Use the remote video camera to sneak up on a hermit crab. Feel one in the touch pool. Did you know jellyfish aren't really fish at all? They float through life with no brain, no spine, no bones, and no heart. In fact, they're 95 percent water!

The Oregon State University Hatfield Marine Science Center

FACT:

Each year, commercial fishermen in the Northwest catch millions of pounds of crab, which are eaten by people across the country. You might like to try crabbing. You'll have to go to a bait shop and rent a crab ring, a round metal trap that looks like a basket. Don't forget the bait!

nearby on Yaquina Bay is another great place to find answers to your questions about the local sea life. The many marine scientists working here study sea life. There is a touch pool, as well as fascinating sea creatures to look at. Don't miss the giant Pacific octopus—it's really ugly! Each of its arms is covered with a double row of suction cups. Octopuses sleep all day and comb the seafloor at night for food.

FACT:

Seals have no visible ears, and when on land they crawl on their bellies. Sea lions have earflaps and walk on all fours.

Many people head north from Newport to Depoe Bay, the tiniest harbor in the world, to watch a few whales. Stop at Devil's Punch Bowl to see huge, crashing waves.

Feel all that wind? No wonder kids are always flying kites along the coast. In fact, a lot of kites are made right here in a factory in Lincoln City. You can tell your friends you were in the "Kite Capital of the World."

Got a kite? What are you waiting for? Race that wind!

KIDS! TELL YOUR PARENTS:

The Oregon Coast offers opportunities for you and your parents to do things you might not be able to do back home. Allow plenty of time for exploring tide pools and flying kites. Rent a ring for a few hours and try crabbing. Stores near the Oregon Dunes sell inexpensive plastic disks for "sledding" on the sand, as well as pails and shovels.

If possible, visit the Oregon Coast Aquarium (503-867-3474) or the Hatfield Marine Science Center (503-867-0100) *before* heading to the beach. That way, you will be able to recognize the sea creatures you'll see once you're actually at the ocean.

Call 800-547-7842 for the *Official Oregon Travel Guide.*

For information on the Oregon Dunes National Recreation Area, call 503-271-3611. There's a visitors center at Reddsport. One good bet for dune buggy tours is Sandland Adventures in Florence; call 503-997-8087. To find out about the Sea Lion Caves, call 503-547-3111.

How many animals and birds did you see at the beaches and aquariums? Make a list of them here, or draw their pictures.

he Chief of the Below World rushed up through the opening in
his mountain, stood on top, and began to hurl fire down on the
people. The Chief of the Above World defended them. The two
chiefs fought a furious battle, throwing red-hot rocks as large as
hills, and causing great landslides of fire. Finally the Chief of the

Above World pushed the Chief of the Below World back into the mountain. When the sun rose, the mountain was gone: it had fallen in on the angry spirit, and all that was left was a large hole. Then the rains came, filling it up.

That's one Native American explanation for how Crater Lake was formed. Of course, scientists tell a much different story.

Crater Lake is the deepest lake in the United States—1,932 feet!—and among the clearest in the world. It was formed 7,700 years ago when a volcano erupted so violently that the top collapsed, leaving a giant crater. Volcanoes are formed when gases deep under the earth's surface explode, pushing out lava (liquid rock), ash, and other materials. Eventually, the crater filled with water from rain and melting snow. No streams or rivers flow in or out of Crater Lake. It's inside the top of the ancient, dormant volcano.

In the summer there are two-hour

FACT:

Peregrine falcons are among the fastest birds in the world, diving at speeds up to 200 miles per hour. Because peregrines are in danger of becoming extinct, scientists are glad there are many nesting at Crater Lake.

boat tours of Crater Lake that are lots of fun. Be prepared for the steep climb down the Cleetwood Trail to the edge of the lake. And be sure to take your own food and water.

But it's worth the trouble. On the boat tour, you'll be able to hike to the top of Wizard Island, a lava dome that was formed after the top of Mount Mazama fell in. It sticks up 760 feet out of the water, and at the top is a 90-foot crater. An Oregon newspaper editor named Crater Lake after the small crater at the top of Wizard Island.

It's spectacular and kind of spooky at the same time to be inside a volcano in the middle of a lake. And speaking of spooky, take a good look at the rock formation called Phantom Ship. You can see it from the boat tour. It's formed of lava and looks kind of like a sailing ship. Can you make out the sails in the rock?

Many people come to Crater Lake in the summer to hike and camp and in the winter to cross-country ski. Hundreds of inches of snow fall here every winter, but the lake rarely freezes. The last time it froze was in 1949.

FACT:

Caldera is the Spanish word for "kettle." Geologists, or scientists who study rocks, use the word to describe big basin-shaped volcanic craters, such as the one that contains Crater Lake.

FACT:

There are more than 600 active volcanoes around the world. Many others are considered dormant, or quiet, but could erupt at any time. Extinct volcanoes are those that have not been active for thousands of years.

There are about 90 miles of hiking trails around Crater Lake. On them, you can see a lot of animals, such as deer, rabbits, frogs, and birds. Look for lizards near the water. For those who like wildflowers, there are two long hikes, one to Annie Creek Canyon and the other to Garfield Peak. Castle Crest Wildflower Trail is a shorter hike. Be sure to stay on the trails. Shortcutting around switchbacks can badly damage slopes and flowers. Whenever you hike, don't take any rocks. If every person who visited Crater Lake pocketed a rock, there wouldn't be any left.

Ready to switch gears entirely? Then head for Ashland, to the south and west of Crater Lake. People from all over the United States come to the Oregon Shakespeare Festival, which takes place every summer in Ashland. You'll enjoy watching William Shakespeare's plays, as parents and kids have for centuries. It's a good idea to try to learn something beforehand about the play you're going to see.

RAFTING

This is more exciting than any roller coaster. You fly over crashing rapids, bouncing up and down and holding on to the side of your boat. Just when you think you can't take any more, the waters calm and you float lazily along, taking pictures, watching animals. You might camp on the river's edge, fish for supper, and swim by the riverbank. Talk about getting away from it all.

That's what river rafting is about. This isn't a sport for young kids: for most trips, guides recommend that rafters be at least 8 years old. Older kids can enjoy rafting, whether it's for an afternoon or a whole week. The rushing rivers of the Northwest, including the Rogue and the Klamath in Oregon, are famous for rafting. Don't forget the sunscreen.

You can take a backstage tour to see how the sets are built, and visit the Exhibit Center, which is full of elaborate costumes from the

productions. At night, festival performers present songs and dances from Old England in the courtyard of the Elizabethan Theatre. Stop at Lithia Park in the middle of Ashland to relax a while.

Everyone in the family will enjoy Ashland's new Pacific Northwest Museum of Natural History. There are exhibits on forests and volcanoes and wildlife from this region, complete with hands-on computer activities. Did you know it would take a 100-foot-tall tree to make all of the wooden things used by just one American each year? See how mice help a forest grow, or walk through a reconstructed lava tube. (You can see a real one at Mount St. Helens.)

You even can learn about detectives who concentrate on solving crimes against wildlife, such as killing deer out of season. How are you at solving mysteries?

To explore more mysterious places, head east of Ashland to Oregon Caves National Monument, near Cave Junction. More than 100 years ago, a local deer hunter following his dog discovered these caves.

ECO SMARTS

Rangers say that you can help protect beautiful places like Crater Lake and even improve the environment at home.

- Pick up litter when you see it.
- Use rechargeable batteries. Disposable batteries are hard on the environment.
- Whenever possible, recycle your paper, plastic, and aluminum.
- Don't buy things that come in a lot of packaging.
- Use less water when brushing your teeth and showering.
- Plant a tree in your backyard.

Today there are more than 3 miles of passages full of stalagmites, stalactites, and more. Don't miss the Ghost Room. It's 250 feet long! See any ghosts?

KIDS! TELL YOUR PARENTS:

The best way to learn about nature is to take your time. Don't rush things! Read about the places you visit before you get there. Go to the visitors center and ask questions. Consider participating in the special programs sometimes offered for kids and families. It's more fun for everyone if parents get involved with their kids learning the names of wildflowers and looking for animals.

To get the most out of a trip to the theater, read about the play or its author beforehand. You'll enjoy a music festival more if you listen to the music on tape before the concert

For information about Crater Lake, call 503-594-2211.

Call the Oregon Caves National Monument at 503-592-2100.

To find out what works will be staged at the Oregon Shakespeare Festival, call 503-482-4331. Phone the Pacific Northwest Museum of Natural History at 503-488-1084.

HIDDEN WORDS

Can you find the following Crater Lake attractions in the grid below? They may appear forward or backward, up or down, or diagonally.

ANNIE CREEK CANYON

CASTLE CREST

CLEETWOOD TRAIL

CRATER LAKE

GARFIELD PEAK

GHOST ROOM

KLAMATH RIVER

PHANTOM SHIP

ROGUE RIVER

WILDLIFE

WIZARD ISLAND

```
Y M P W I Z A R D I S L A N D U
N P S D O X C O F V B T O A H J
T H R O M E A G T I L K Y F E K
G A X A I N S U P A V L C W V L
A N N I E C R E E K C A N Y O N
R T Q D V G X R U F S M L X C G
F O V L C K N I D T D A C U D H
I M H B R S W V L O Y T F Z O O
E S C R B K Z E A C T H U M O S
L H I Q W G C R Y P H R Y S W T
D I J N R R D G O J Q I M H T R
P P S I E O J F Z Q N V P D E O
E B V S P Q R C M Y K E B T E O
A U T E K A L R E T A R C Y L M
K L I A R T D O O W T E E L C M
S W I L D L I F E S M F A R I P
```

(Answers are on page 108)

ancouver, Vancouver, this is it!"

David Johnston, a young government geologist, radioed that message early on May 18, 1980. It was all he had time to say. Johnston was caught in the eruption of the Mount St. Helens volcano and was never found.

Mount St. Helens, quiet for 123 years, had begun waking up 2 months earlier, when scientists realized that the volcano was shooting steam and ash into the sky. There were earthquakes deep in the ground. Hot, molten rock was being squeezed up into the volcano, like toothpaste in a tube. A huge bulge had formed on the north face of the mountain. By April it was growing at the rate of five feet a day.

But no one was prepared for what happened the Sunday morning Mount St. Helens erupted. Liquid lava did not flow out. Instead, it started with an earthquake that triggered a huge avalanche, a mass of earth that suddenly slid down the mountain, mowing over everything in its path. At the east of Mount St. Helens, Spirit Lake was completely

FACT:

Scientists use a seismograph to find and record movements within the earth. This machine also tells them how strong an earthquake is. Sometimes an earthquake is a warning that a volcano is preparing to erupt.

FACT:

The Yakima Indian Nation called Mount St. Helens "Lawalitetlah," which means "Fire Mountain." Many Native American legends warned of its dangers.

filled in by the avalanche. A hot wind blew across the land, carrying stones. A 12-mile ash cloud shot into the air, darkening the sky. Eventually, this cloud circled the earth. People in nearby towns had to shovel ash like snow, but it was a lot harder to get rid of.

Floods of water mixed with chunks of land rushed into streams and rivers, washing away homes, cars, and bridges that kids crossed every day to get to school. Super-hot rock shot out of the volcano later in the day and flowed across the land. Thirty-six people and thousands of animals died.

The blast zoomed through 230 square miles of forest. It could take 200 years for the trees to grow back. The land around the mountain was covered with craters and looked like a moonscape.

Now the mountain is 8,365 feet high—1,300 feet shorter than before it erupted—and there is a 2,000-foot-deep crater below the rim. But the volcano didn't really blow its top. Rather, the mountain exploded sideways. To understand volcanoes, think of the earth's surface as solid rock, a thick jigsaw of continents and ocean floors. Beneath this surface, the earth is so hot it's liquid, containing gases that are always exploding and trying to escape. The word "volcano"

A Native American Love Story

An old woman named Loowit once guarded a fire that happened to be the only fire in the world. As her reward, the Great Spirit Tamanwit gave her eternal life. When she complained that she didn't want to be old and ugly forever, he made her young and beautiful.

But then his sons, Wy'East and Pahto, fell in love with Loowit and fought for her, burning forests and villages. Tamanwit was so angry that he killed the 3 of them and created a mountain peak where each had fallen. Loowit is Mount St. Helens, still guarding the fire. Wy'East is Mount Hood, lifting his head proudly. Pahto became Mount Adams, his head bent in sorrow.

comes from Vulcan, the Roman god of fire and the forge.

Before the eruption, Mount St. Helens was one of the most beautiful and popular spots for hiking, camping, and fishing in the Northwest. If you go to Mount St. Helens National Volcanic Monument today, you will see an area that is slowly recovering. The mountain is huge, and roads don't cross it or connect conveniently, so you will have to hike on trails to get a good look at it.

On the east side of the mountain, at Windy Ridge, take the Truman Trail to get the closest view of the lava dome.

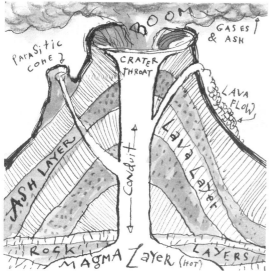

The 1-mile Harmony Trail is the only way to get to Spirit Lake now. Stay off the floating logs. They can be dangerous.

People also like to take the Lava Canyon Trail over the Muddy River to see waterfalls. Watch out for slippery rocks!

Take the Winds of Change Trail outside the Coldwater Ridge

Visitor Center and you'll feel like you're on another planet. Dead trees are strewn around like toothpicks. Notice all of the mounds of rock and mud. They're called "hummocks."

Naturalists lead walks along the Winds of Change Trail, and point out how plants and animals survived the eruption. Gophers, for instance, buried themselves underground; ants found hiding places in logs; and frogs burrowed deep in lakes.

Plants that seemed to die after the eruption have started growing again. Animals that were not seen after the blast, such as elk and deer, have returned. And birds began flying back as soon as the ash settled. Hike the Meta Lake Trail to see plants and animals that survived the eruption, as well as those that returned afterward.

At the National Monument, 110,000 acres have been set aside

APE CAVE

It's dark and slimy and has been here for 1,900 years. Ape Cave is really a 2¼-mile-long lava tube that was formed during a volcanic eruption. Lava from the eruption cooled and hardened, forming a cylinder, while hot lava from the same eruption continued to flow through it. When the hot lava flow stopped, a hollow tube had been created.

You can hike through Ape Cave in Mount St. Helens National Volcanic Monument. Don't forget a flashlight.

so people can study the ways nature heals itself.

Scientists are doing all they can to help the recovery. Nearly 10 million trees have been planted. Take a walk along the shore of Coldwater Lake. It's a good place for a picnic. At the Discovery Area you can skip on stones and balance on logs.

When will Mount St. Helens erupt again? No one really knows. But one thing is sure—scientists are watching very carefully.

KIDS! TELL YOUR PARENTS:

The drive to Mount St. Helens can be long and winding. If you feel yourself getting carsick, keep a window open to let fresh air in. Play a story tape or listen to some music. But don't read. The idea is to look around, not down. Eat lightly. Ask your doctor about medicine to prevent motion sickness.

For more information about Mount St. Helens National Volcanic Monument, call 206-750-3900. Camping is not allowed at the monument, but campsites are located within an hour's drive. Read *Fire Mountain,* a good introduction on the volcano for the entire family. This book is available, along with others, at the visitors center. Call 206-274-2100.

eam up to the top of the huge flying saucer and check out that view!

Seattle's Space Needle isn't a real flying saucer. But it sure looks like one standing on stilts.

The Space Needle was built for the 1962 World's Fair and is 605 feet high. The view is so great that many visitors to Seattle, Washington, head here first. It's fun to zoom up to the top in the super-fast elevator. It goes 10 miles per hour.

From the top, you can see the entire city and beyond—skyscrapers and parks, houses, mountains, and, of course, water. Much of Seattle is surrounded by it. There is freshwater Lake Washington to the east and saltwater

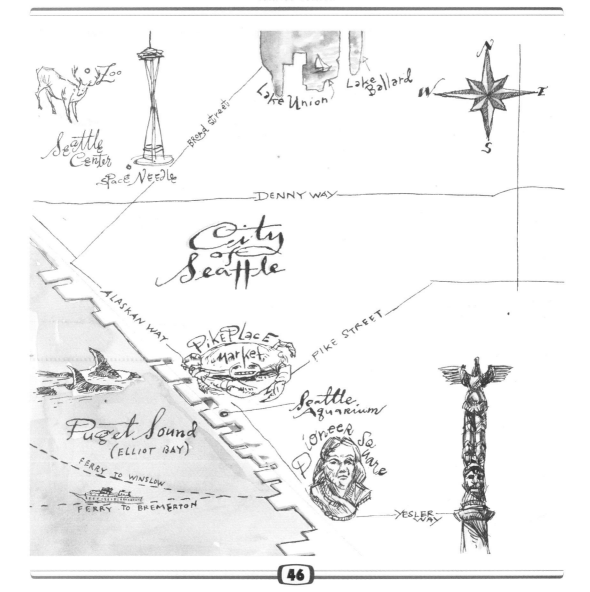

Puget Sound to the west.

You can see snowcapped mountains, too. When people in Seattle say "the mountain is out," they mean that the weather is so clear they can see Mount Rainier. Try out the high-powered telescopes. How many different kinds of boats can you spot? One of the reasons Seattle is famous for its restaurants is all of the fish in the water. Have you ever eaten fresh salmon? Kids in Seattle eat it all the time.

Besides boating and fishing, there are lots of other outdoor activities in Seattle. Many families here go skiing on slopes less than an hour's drive from the city. Or they can visit a foreign country just for the day—Canada is only 113 miles away. You'll see parents and kids riding bikes everywhere, even to work. There are 40 miles of trails in the city. Everyone wears a bike helmet. It's the law.

After you've looked down on Seattle from the Space Needle,

FACT:

In 1851, settlers named Seattle after Sealth, a local Native American chief who had become their friend.

Take Flight

Did you arrive in Seattle by plane? Just a few miles from the airport is Seattle's Museum of Flight, which displays planes from throughout the history of aviation. More than 50 full-size aircraft hang from the ceiling in formation, 6 stories above the ground. There are biplanes, seaplanes, and fighter jets. Climb into a model of an F-18 jet fighter. See how planes are readied for flight in the hangar. There is even a moon rock in the *Apollo* exhibit.

If you're 10 or older, go to nearby Everett, where you can see how planes are built at the world's largest aircraft manufacturing plant: Boeing. After taking his first flight in 1916, a young Seattle lumberman named Bill Boeing decided he could make better planes. Today, Boeing is the leading airplane manufacturer in the world.

you'll be ready to begin exploring the 74-acre Seattle Center. The Space Needle, the city's most famous landmark, is right in the middle, and there are more things for kids to do at the Seattle Center than there is time to do them.

Look for the life-size green dinosaurs. They're made of 7,000 ivy plants and thousands of pounds of moss.

How about a play or a concert? The Seattle Children's Theatre is headquartered here, along with the Seattle Symphony, the

Seattle Youth Symphony, the Seattle Opera, the Pacific Northwest Ballet, and other fine arts groups. There are thousands of performances all year long, including a lot of rock concerts.

At the Seattle Center Coliseum, you can watch an NBA basketball game played by the Seattle Supersonics or an NHL hockey game with the Seattle Thunderbirds.

Hop aboard the sleek white monorail at the Seattle Center any time of year for an incredible 90-second ride above the city. It has traveled more than 1.3 million miles since it was built for the 1962 World's Fair—that's over two trips to the moon and back. (Sit in the front seat, if you can!)

Next head for the big white arches of the Pacific

Science Center, also located in the Seattle Center. You could easily spend all day exploring its 5 floors. Try shooting the huge water cannons at targets in the fountains outside—the targets turn when you hit them. If you're tall enough, ride the high-rail bike in a circle 12 feet above the ground—you won't fall!

Try playing virtual basketball at the Tech Zone, in the Science

BOAT COUNTRY

One out of 5 Seattleites owns some kind of boat. A good place to see boats close-up is the Hiram M. Chittenden Locks in Ballard, just 5 miles from Seattle Center.

The locks serve as a water elevator, raising and lowering small kayaks, fishing boats, and Coast Guard cutters traveling between saltwater Puget Sound and freshwater Lake Union. More than 60,000 boats pass through the locks each year. The water level of Lake Union can reach as much as 26 feet higher than that of the Sound. In the summer, you might see dozens of boats waiting to get through.

Here's how it works: The boats enter the locks a few at a time. The steel gates close behind them, and water from the ship canal is allowed to flow in. When the boats have been raised by the incoming water to the level of Lake Union, they can move forward into Salmon Bay and then into the lake. The process is reversed for boats heading into Puget Sound.

Center. Put on the special virtual reality glove. Move your arm, and the on-screen ball moves with it. It's all done with computers. When you're ready for the next challenge, try beating a 10-foot-tall robot at ticktacktoe or designing a newsletter on a computer. Play music in Sound Sensations. Or experiment on yourself in Body Work: Can your hand pump blood as well as your heart? Elsewhere in the museum, freeze shadows on the wall and meet robot dinosaurs.

FACT:

Seattle gets 37.1 inches of rain each year. Despite the city's soggy reputation, that's less than Atlanta, Boston, New York, and Houston.

At the Willard W. Smith Planetarium in the Science Center, you can search for stars.

The Children's Museum is just across the courtyard, downstairs in the Center House. Here you can play in the Little Lagoon or add on to the pipe structure in Pipe Dreams. Can you tell where the balls you drop will come out of the maze? Visit the museum's "neighborhood" designed just for kids and stop in across the hall at the Imagination Station. You might have a chance to create an art project with help from a professional artist.

There's plenty to do outside, too, especially in warm weather. Turn a few cartwheels. Get your face painted. In a few steps you can be at the Fun Forest, complete with rides, cotton candy, arcade games, and even miniature golf. You can ride bumper cars or take a flight to Mars. Or take a ride on the merry-go-round with your younger brothers and sisters.

Are you in the mood to talk to the animals? You'll find plenty of them at Seattle's Woodland Park Zoo, a short drive north from the Seattle Center. There's no better place to meet a few gorillas, giraffes, snow leopards, and bald eagles, along with dozens of other creatures. The Woodland Park Zoo is one of the nation's best and is famous for re-creating the natural habitats of its animals. Visit the gorillas' rain forest. Don't miss the savanna, where you can see lions, zebras, and elephants roaming the countryside as they would in Africa. Don't worry, there are hidden barriers. Take the new Northern Trail. Do you see a bear fishing for salmon?

KIDS! TELL YOUR PARENTS:

Seattle is a great city for kids. There is so much to see and do in the museums and at the zoo that it's impossible to take it all in. Don't rush through everything. Instead, choose a few exhibits and spend plenty of time at each one. If you and your brothers and sisters are different ages and you have two adults with you, split up for a while so each group can see what they want to. Don't forget to carry snacks and a water bottle.

To plan a trip to Seattle, call the Seattle/King County Convention & Visitors Bureau at 206-461-5840. For information on the Boeing plant tour, call 206-342-4801.

Ultimate Washington, from the editors at Ulysses Press, is a good travel guide for your parents.

CROSSWORD PUZZLE

Across

2. Seattle's basketballers.

4. A type of boat.

8. Sticky stuff invented in Seattle.

9. Kind of crab.

Down

1. Two-wheeled vehicles.

2. City in the Northwest United States.

3. Famous Seattle landmark.

5. Exhibit with moon rocks.

6. _____ Sound.

7. Used for air travel.

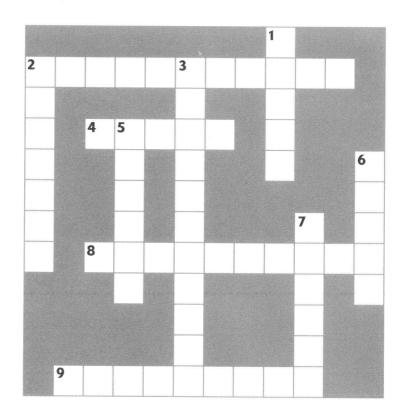

(Answers are on page 110)

on't bother with breakfast. Go directly to Pike Place Market.

You won't go hungry.

There's so much food that the only problem is deciding what to eat: a Washington apple or some yellow Rainier cherries, a flavored

honey stick, a home-baked cookie, fish-and-chips, hazelnuts, or eggs and muffins at the famous Lowell's Restaurant.

In 1907 Pike Place Market was established so farmers could bring their produce to Seattle and sell it directly to the people who lived there. The market was a big success until the 1940s. But when World War II began, many Japanese-American farmers were forced off their farms and into internment camps. The market lost nearly half its farmers.

After the war, many families moved to the suburbs and stopped shopping at Pike Place Market. Eventually, businesses wanted to tear the market down and add new buildings. But many Seattleites fought to preserve it. The market has been entirely renovated, and is now as important to the city as the Space Needle. Nine million people visit it every year! Local schoolkids come for field trips.

The market's tables are piled high with whatever fruits and vegetables are in season, like peaches, apricots, Chinese vegetables, and, of course, apples. Did you know Washington grows more apples than any other state? Most people's favorite apple is the red delicious. Washington is known for its seafood, too. The state's fishermen harvest more than 2.3 billion pounds of fish and seafood every year. Huge, glistening salmon, halibut, mussels, and shrimp are sold at the market. Here's your chance to get a close-up look at those famous

FLOATING HIGHWAY

It's a tourist attraction, a seagoing bus, and a kind of highway all rolled into one. Washington State Ferries is the biggest ferry system in the U.S., transporting more than 20 million people across Puget Sound each year.

People take their cars, trucks, bikes, campers, even canoes and kayaks aboard. Others simply walk on. Birthday parties, weddings, and other celebrations are held on the ferries.

For kids, riding a ferry is certainly a lot more fun than spending hours in the back seat of a car. But sometimes changing tides can disrupt ferry schedules—then you will have to wait. So bring along a good book or a deck of cards!

Dungeness crabs. If you see a fish or a vegetable you don't recognize, ask the person who's selling it. That's how you become part of the old "meet the producer" tradition—buying and learning directly from farmers and fishermen. Ask them where they come from. They're from all over the state.

Many craftspeople sell their wares at Pike Place Market, too, making this a first-rate place to buy souvenirs: rocks, T-shirts and posters, earrings and hair ribbons, hats, and all kinds of other crafts. Need some shades? Even though the sun doesn't often shine here, Seattleites are said to buy more sunglasses than people in any other American city!

Don't miss Rachel the pig, a gigantic bronze piggy bank under the clock at the market. People drop money in Rachel, as much as $9,000 each year, to help support programs for neighborhood residents.

Did you notice the Sanitary Market

FACT:

There are mountains on both sides of Seattle: the Cascades to the east and the Olympics to the west. The city was built on 7 hills, but today there are only 6. Around the turn of the century, Denny Hill was leveled by gigantic water hoses to make way for new houses.

building? It got its name because it was the only building in the market where animals weren't allowed.

Now look at the floor. There are more than 46,000 names sandblasted on the tiles of the market's arcades. Ten years ago, each of these people donated $35 to repair the floor. Can you find former President Reagan's tile?

A short stroll from the market brings you to the Seattle Art Museum, whose exhibits include African masks, Northwest Native American art, and photographs. Be sure to see the huge sculpture of *The Hammering Man* outside.

The waterfront is not far from Pike Place Market, either. To reach it, you can go down several flights of stairs known as the "Hillclimb." Once at the waterfront, the Waterfront Trolley is a good way to get around. You'll find more shops and restaurants here than fishermen!

FACT:

Seattleites have a surefire method for spotting tourists: they look for jaywalkers. Jaywalking—which means crossing the street at a place where there's no crosswalk—is illegal in most of Seattle. Pike Place Market is one place where it's allowed.

Take the trolley to Pioneer Square, the first part of Seattle to be settled. It grew rapidly during the Klondike gold rush of 1897.

Hearing stories of gold in the Klondike region of Canada, many Seattleites, including the mayor, immediately quit their jobs and headed for Canada to dig for the precious metal. More than 9,000 people and 36,000 tons of supplies left Seattle during the

LOOK AT THEM GO!

Could you find your way back to the place you were born with just your nose to guide you? Salmon do.

For the first several months of their lives, salmon remain in the freshwater streams where they were born, feeding and growing strong. Then they head downstream to the ocean, where they live for up to 4 years.

When it's time to spawn, or lay their eggs, they return home, sometimes swimming over 1,000 miles.

Chinook are the largest salmon and the most prized by people who fish. Coho are silvery and turn purplish-red during spawning. Sockeye males turn red at mating time.

Each female salmon lays up to 5,000 eggs. But most of the young fish don't survive. Scientists are very concerned because fewer and fewer salmon are making it back to their spawning grounds. Fish ladders and egg hatcheries have been built to help the salmon.

first 6 weeks of the gold rush.

Few who set out for the goldfields struck it rich. But Seattle was never the same. The Klondike gold rush transformed Seattle into a major city, as businesses sprang up to supply gold-seekers with the equipment and services they needed.

Did you know the term "skid row" started right here in Seattle? Yesler Way, in the heart of Pioneer Square, is the original skid row, down which logs were "skidded" to the sawmill.

While in Pioneer Square, find out more about the gold rush at the Klondike Gold Rush National Historical Park, on the site where prospectors bought their supplies and boarded ships for the gold country. You can buy your own gold nugget there. Stop in at Ruby Montana's Pinto Pony on Second Avenue to buy other treasures.

Then join the Underground Tour at Doc Maynard's Public House around the block to see the city's original streets. They are underground. In Seattle's early days, the streets were constantly being flooded by the rising tides of the sea. Kids would raft down the streets. After the entire downtown was destroyed by a fire in 1889, city leaders decided to solve the flooding problem by rebuilding the downtown streets a full story higher. What do you think about the hollow sidewalks?

Farther along the waterfront is the Seattle Aquarium. This is where you can find out everything you want to know about salmon and the other sea life from nearby waters. Did you know that the largest octopus in the entire world, the giant Pacific octopus, lives in Puget Sound?

Walk through the aquarium's Underwater Dome to see Puget Sound from the viewpoint of a fish. More than 200 animals live in the 400,000-gallon tank in cold, salty water, just as they do in the sound.

Stop by the Touch Tank to hold starfish and featherduster worms, among other slippery, slimy creatures. Twenty kinds of starfish live in Puget Sound, including the sunflower star, the biggest in the world. It can have up to 24 arms!

After you have seen the salmon outside, count the colors on the tropical fish in the Pacific Coral Reef. Then see the tiny jellyfish through a giant video microscope in the Discovery Lab. The ocean will never look the same to you again.

KIDS! TELL YOUR PARENTS:

Riding the Washington State Ferries is a lot of fun, but because of the crowds it can also be frustrating. It's important to plan ahead, especially in the summer and on weekends. Try to avoid commuter hours (eastbound in the morning and westbound in the evening) and arrive early. It's not uncommon for people to line up 2 hours or more ahead of time. Even so, you still might have to wait for the next sailing. If you're traveling between Anacortes or the San Juan Islands to Sidney, British Columbia, you may make a courtesy reservation for your car. For schedules and information, call 206-464-6400 (from within Washington, 800-84-FERRY).

Call Pike Place Market at 206-682-7453, and the Seattle Aquarium at 206-386-4300. For more information about the Underground Tour call 206-682-1511. Reach the Klondike Gold Rush National Historical Park at 206-553-7220.

WORD JUMBLE

Unscramble the letters to spell the names of things you can buy on Seattle's waterfront. The shaded squares will tell you the name of this place.

1. lpaep

2. itbuahl

3. neohy ctiks

4. hrisecre

5. rmihps

6. elforws

7. laicrg

8. chepa

9. lleejynabs

10. modasln

11. bacr

12. tocirpa

13. kooiecs

14. leyjl

15. zelhautn

(Answers are on page 108)

o climb a mountain. Or at least part of a mountain. There's
no better place to try than Mount Rainier.

Each year, 4,500 people climb to the 14,411-foot-high summit
of Mount Rainier. Almost the same number of people try to climb
to the top but don't make it. Thousands more come just to hike and

enjoy Mount Rainier National Park.

Almost all American mountaineering expeditions train here before attempting to scale the world's tallest peaks. Men and women have been trying to conquer Mount Rainier's icy slopes for more than 100 years.

FACT:

Native Americans believed Mount Rainier, which they called "Tahoma," was home to a god who showered fire, rocks, and snow down on their villages when he got angry. That's why they never went near the summit.

In 1870 Hazard Stevens and Philemon Beecher Van Trump found themselves stranded near the summit at night with a storm approaching. If they hadn't discovered ice caves where they could take shelter, they probably wouldn't have survived to become the first climbers to reach the top.

In those days climbers didn't have much equipment to help them. They had to pound nails into their shoes to make hiking boots. In 1890 a teacher named Fay Fuller became the first woman to reach the summit. She climbed while wearing a long wool skirt!

Today, you will see climbers using the latest high-tech equipment. They have traveled around the world and across the United States for a chance to climb this mountain. Some kids climb with their parents.

Mountain climbing is no walk in the meadow, though. It's serious business. Many climbers say they got started by hiking a lot when they were kids. So what are you waiting for?

At Mount Rainier there are more than 300 miles of hiking trails, some winding through old growth forests. These forests have large live trees (some more than 1,000 years old), dead tree logs, and all kinds of ferns, vines, mosses, and plants. The dead trees become homes for animals and seedbeds for new trees and shrubs. Hike through meadows studded with wildflowers to lakes and waterfalls. You can even hike to where you'll see glaciers, sometimes called "moving rivers of ice."

LAND OF ICE

Glaciers are formed when the winter snowfall is so great that it can't all melt during the warmer months. The unmelted snow accumulates day after day, month after month. Eventually, it turns into ice and pushes its way down the mountain. Glaciers may not look as if they are moving, but they are, constantly.

How fast do they go? That depends on how much snow has fallen. Mount Rainier's glaciers sometimes move 2 feet a day, cutting great cracks called crevasses into the mountainside, and grinding rock beneath them into a "flour" that makes the streams look dirty.

There are 25 named glaciers and 50 small, unnamed glaciers on the slopes of Mount Rainier. Emmons Glacier is the biggest.

Before setting out, stop by one of the visitors centers in the Paradise Valley, Longmire, Sunrise, and Ohanapecosh areas of the park. They've got touch tables. Have you ever touched a deer antler? Rangers there can tell you where to find the most fun hiking trails. Ask the rangers about their special Junior Ranger programs for kids.

The Wonderland Trail circles the mountain—it's 93 miles long! To see a glacier close-up, take the 7-mile Carbon River Trail along Carbon River. Hike the 1.2-mile Nisqually Vista Trail. The altitude is

so high you may be hiking through clouds. Or explore the 1.5-mile Grove of the Patriarchs Trail, which winds through towering Douglas fir trees on an island in the Ohanapecosh River.

Have you ever seen the top of a waterfall? Hike up the Comet Falls Trail to see falls that plunge 320 feet. Two of the falls are named after people (Myrtle Falls, for someone who climbed the mountain years ago, and Carter Falls, to honor an early guide).

HIKING SMARTS

Here are some tips from rangers to keep you safe on the trail:

- Stay on the trail.

- Never hike alone. Keep track of everyone in your group.

- Wear sturdy, comfortable shoes with heavy socks.

- Always carry rain gear, a jacket, food, and water. Don't drink the water in rivers and streams.

- Don't swim above waterfalls or jump from rock to rock near the edges of streams and rivers.

- If someone gets hurt, send one person ahead for help. Write down your location and the age, height, and weight of the injured hiker, so the rangers will know what equipment to bring.

- Stash a flashlight and batteries, a first aid kit, waterproof matches, and a pencil and paper in an adult's backpack.

There's also Spray Falls on Spray Creek, among others. Ask a ranger to steer you toward trails near the falls.

Whichever trail you take, be sure to look out for wildflowers, which begin blooming very early in spring, even before the snow melts, and continue through the summer. Keep an eye open for blue lupine, red Indian paintbrush, and purple Jeffrey's shooting star. How many kinds of wildflowers can you find? Be careful where you walk. If you trample them, they may not bloom again for years. That's why rangers ask you to stay on the trails.

Because Mount Rainier is such a popular spot for camping and fishing, the park is often crowded all summer. Many families prefer to head north along the Cascade Range to Mount Baker and North Cascades National Park. While you're there, you can take a boat trip up Lake Chelan or raft down the Stehekin River.

Wherever you are in the fall, look for the different mushrooms growing on the forest floor. Don't eat them! Some are poisonous. But help yourself to some huckleberries—they're delicious!

Many families like to go to Mount Rainier in the winter for cross-country skiing and snowshoeing. Paradise Valley has become the center for winter action. It gets 630 inches of snow a year!

No matter what the season is, you're likely to see animals. Keep your eyes peeled for mountain goats, chipmunks, owls and other birds, elk, deer, moose, and snowshoe rabbits, which are brown in the summer but turn white in the winter. As you walk, look for animal footprints.

When you're finished exploring Mount Rainier, head for Eatonville and Northwest Trek, a 600-acre wildlife park, to see all the animals you may have missed—or wanted to avoid—in your visits to the national parks of the Northwest.

You can stare down a wolf, get face-to-face with a grizzly, watch a black bear splash in the water, or see a bald eagle perched in a tree. It's not dangerous; they're all behind barriers.

Take a tram tour and see bison, elk, and mountain goats roam. Don't miss the wolves. They live in packs—groups of families with

parents and kids. Stop at the Cheney Discovery Center for plenty of hands-on action.

Has anyone ever said you eat like a moose? Next time, tell them that's impossible. A moose eats 27,000 calories a day. To match that, you would have to eat 42 Big Macs!

KIDS! TELL YOUR PARENTS:

You may get bored and hungry while hiking. To avoid this, plan shorter hikes. Ask rangers to suggest trails that are just right for you. And always carry snacks and lots of water. If the going gets rough, sing songs or stage a contest to see who can spot the most animals or flowers.

Call Mount Rainier National Park at 206 569-2211 for general questions and camping information. For lodging reservations inside the park, call 206-569-2275. For info on climbing and guide services, call 206-569-2227 (in the summer) and 206-627-6242 (in the winter).

To reach North Cascades National Park, phone 206-386-4495. Call Northwest Trek at 206-832-6122.

The Northwest Interpretive Association offers many books that will help you plan your visit. *A Traveler's Companion to Mount Rainier National Monument* is one good bet. To order a catalog, call 206-220-4140.

o you like water? Then Olympic National Park is the place for
you. Soak in hot mineral pools, fish in icy glacier-carved
lakes, climb to see waterfalls, and explore tide pools at the ocean's
edge. You can also hike up a mountain trail around Hurricane
Ridge amid the wildflowers for a spectacular look at the snow-

covered Olympic Mountains.

Many people think Olympic National Park is like 3 parks in one. That's because within its 900,000 acres there are high mountains, ocean beaches, and rain forests.

You'll feel like you're in another world as you tromp through the Hoh Rain Forest on the west side of the park. In this dense green growth, every inch of space is occupied by plants. Some of the trees, covered with moss and ferns, resemble giant green monsters.

Olympic National Park has 3 rain forests within its borders: the Hoh, the Queets, and the

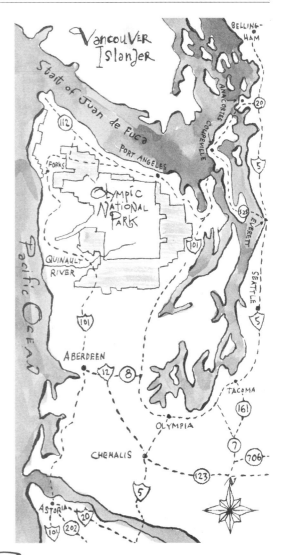

Quinault. Rain forests are unusual in temperate climates such as this. They are found only in New Zealand, Chile, and here, along the Northwest coast, where the weather is neither very hot nor very cold and there's lots of rain and fog. The Hoh Rain Forest gets 12 feet of rain a year, in one long, wet season. Tropical rain forests, on the other hand, get rain year-round and the weather is much hotter.

FACT:

Eleven Native American tribes live throughout the Olympic Peninsula. They practice traditional crafts—wood carving, weaving, and basketry—just as they have for generations.

To explore the Hoh Rain Forest, take the Hall of Mosses Trail or the slightly longer Spruce Nature Trail and look for the huge Sitka spruce trees. You'll know you've found them when you see trees that look like they're on stilts. Sitkas grow in rows that are called colonnades. Temperate rain forests are known for these rows of trees, which are among the tallest in the world.

Animals live here, too. There are deer, squirrels, elk, and birds. Even yellow banana slugs. They like to eat mushrooms, no matter what they're called!

ANIMAL SMARTS

According to rangers, these tips will help you spot animals while you hike:

- Move slowly so you don't startle them.

- Watch from a distance. Carry binoculars.

- Be quiet. Loud noises scare animals.

- Avoid crowds.

- Do not disturb nesting areas.

- Be patient. Sometimes your presence will make them leave, but if they don't sense danger they might come back.

- Don't approach the animals. They're wild. And never feed them—it's not safe for you or the animals.

You'll also see experienced mountain climbers hiking in the Hoh Rain Forest. That's because it provides the shortest route to Blue Glacier and up the 7,965-foot Mount Olympus, the highest point in Olympic National Park.

There are about 60 glaciers in the Olympic Mountains. The Blue and the Anderson glaciers are visited more than any others in the park.

FACT:

One of the reasons Olympic National Park was created was to protect the Roosevelt elk, which was named for President Theodore Roosevelt and is found only in the Northwest. The park was almost called Elk National Park and today is home to the world's largest herd of wild Roosevelt elk.

Ready to hit the beach? Don't forget your shoes. There are plenty of beaches at Olympic National Park, but you have to walk down steep paths to get to them. Between Ruby Beach and Kalaloch Beach there are paths leading down to 6 beaches. Be careful. Sudden high waves can turn drifting logs into dangerous weapons.

Head to northern beaches such as Ozette, where you'll see giant sea stacks sticking up out of the water. Spotted any harbor seals? Sometimes they follow along with you in the water as you hike on the beach. Take the 3⅓-mile Cape Acaoa Trek along a wooden walkway down to Ozette Beach. After you've hiked this trail, you can tell your friends that you reached the westernmost point of land in the lower 48 states.

Take the time to explore the tide pools along the rocks. They are full of all kinds of strange creatures. Ozette Lake, the largest freshwater lake in Washington, is also nearby. It's a good spot for fishing and boating.

Ozette Lake is about 30 miles from the town of Neah Bay, where you can find out about the Native Americans who live in this area—and were here before anyone else. A 500-year-old Makah village has been uncovered by archaeologists, who are specially trained to figure out how people used to live. The village

is not open to tourists, but families can visit the Makah Cultural and Research Center to learn about the Makah way of life. Did you see the totem pole?

From late spring until fall, you can take a dip in the mineral pools at the Sol Duc Hot Springs Resort, farther east in

Olympic National Park. The water is very hot! Some people think it cures all kinds of aches, pains, sprains, and even illnesses. (If you don't want to go into the mineral pools, there is a big swimming pool.) Sol Duc was named by Native Americans who also believed that the water had unusual powers. The words mean "sparkling water." This is a great spot for a lazy summer afternoon.

Another good bet for a lazy day in the park is Lake Crescent, about 15 miles north of Sol Duc. This deep freshwater lake was formed by a glacier. You can take a paddlewheeler cruise out on the lake or hike the 1-mile-long Marymere Falls Trail to see the waterfall. It drops 90 feet.

On your way to or from Olympic National Park, you may pass through Port Townsend. Back when Seattle was a small town, this was a bustling lumber port. Today, much of Port Townsend looks the way it did more than 100 years ago, with well-kept, brightly-painted Victorian homes and buildings. This is a great place to stop for lunch, sightseeing, and shopping—or to learn more about soldiering at Fort Worden State Park's Artillery Museum and Commanding Officer's House.

Got your imagination revved up? Stop in Sequim (pronounced "Skwim") and take a walk through the sand at the Dungeness National Wildlife Refuge. Everyone calls it the Dungeness Spit. It's the longest natural sand spit in the world, stretching for 5½ miles into the Strait of Juan de Fuca, the body of water that separates the Olympic Peninsula from Canada.

Kids love to come here because the beach has gigantic piles of driftwood that can be used to build caves, castles, and hideouts. The beaches are great for building sand castles and for bird-watching, too. More than 250 kinds of birds feed and nest here, including blue herons, swans, gulls, and swallows.

Just down the road is another place to see animals: the Olympic Game Farm. Here, it's OK to feed wild animals. Grab a loaf of bread, ask an adult to drive you through the game farm, and feed llamas and bears, buffalo and zebra from your car window. They are comfortable with people. Many of them have performed in movies and TV shows. Recognize any stars?

KIDS! TELL YOUR PARENTS:

Not everyone likes to shop. So before you set out, the entire family should decide how much time will be spent on shopping.

Talk to your parents about how much money they will give you and how much you can spend from your own savings. Decide what kind of souvenir you want—one very important one or a collection of inexpensive things, such as postcards from all the places you visit. A sparkling rock? A stuffed animal? A poster?

Call Olympic National Park at 206-452-0330. The Olympic Park Institute offers many programs geared toward families; for information, call 206-928-3720. Call the Makah Cultural and Research Center at 206-645-2711, the Dungeness National Wildlife Refuge at 206-457-8451, and the Olympic Game Farm at 206-683-4295. For general information on the area, call the North Olympic Peninsula Visitor & Convention Bureau at 206-452-8552.

Draw a picture of your family having fun at Olympic National Park. What did you like the best?

ot your binoculars ready? You'll find plenty of use for them on the San Juan Islands. If you're lucky, you'll see orca whales swimming by, harbor seals poking their heads out of the water, bald eagles perched on tree branches, sea lions lazing on rocks, and porpoises practicing their water acrobatics.

The San Juan Islands, a group of 172 islands, are located north of Seattle in Puget Sound. They range in size from tiny 1-acre islands to Orcas Island, which is 56 square miles.

Some people call the San Juan Islands "the

KEEP PADDLING

You can paddle around in a kayak just as the Eskimos did thousands of years ago. They traveled all the way up and down the Pacific Coast in their kayaks, which they crafted from wood with animal skins stretched on top.

Today, kayaks are sleek fiberglass vessels, and are even made in sizes that are perfect for kids. They're easier to maneuver in the water and carry on land because they're so light. How are your arm muscles?

Whether you paddle your own kayak or share a larger one with a parent or a guide, there's no better way to explore the San Juan Islands.

It feels as if you're sitting right in the water, as you watch all of the animals and fish swim by. You can stop on any beach and take a dip.

Look out for your camera. It might get wet.

magic islands." They're full of hidden coves and inlets, quiet country roads that are great for biking, and long stretches of beach. Have you ever dug for clams? You can do it here.

You'll need to rent a boat to reach many of the islands. Only a few of the islands have people living on them. Some are wildlife refuges. Waldron Island is home to whistling swans, and little Puffin Island has harbor seals and puffins. While you are on the water, you will see fishermen from all over the world angling for salmon and

FACT:

Male and female bald eagles take care of their young and build huge nests together, often returning to the same one year after year. More than 100 pairs nest in the San Juan Islands.

trout. But that's not all they'll catch. More than 200 kinds of fish swim in these waters.

After arriving on the islands, almost everyone heads first to Friday Harbor on San Juan Island. With 1,500 people living here, it's the islands' only city. There are plenty of restaurants, shops, and places to stay. Try a grilled salmon sandwich.

San Juan Island is as famous for one hungry pig as it is for its sea life. In 1859, this pig almost caused a war between the United States and England. At the time, the two countries were arguing over who controlled the territory.

The trouble started when a San Juan settler shot and killed the pig, which belonged to the British-run Hudson Bay Company. Soon,

FACT:

Sea stars, or starfish, come in nearly every color and many different shapes. Look for orange morning sun stars, purple common stars, green serpent stars, and red brittle stars. They will die if they're left out of the water. When you pick one up, always put it back where you found it.

American soldiers were manning their cannons on one side of the island. More than 2,000 British soldiers came and a stand-off began.

It took 12 years before control of the island was given to the United States. The pig was the only casualty. You can still visit the English and American camps, now part of the San Juan Island National Historic Park. They're on opposite sides of San Juan Island. And you won't find any pigs.

But you will find everything you want to know about orcas at the Whale Museum, the only museum in the country dedicated entirely to whales. Orcas are called killer whales because they eat other warm-blooded animals, such as seals and porpoises. The orcas in

Puget Sound mostly eat fish. Look at the huge whale skeletons. Pick up a phone and listen to whale sounds. See the life-size models hanging from the ceiling. Adult orcas can grow up to 30 feet long. Did you know a whale's pregnancy lasts nearly twice as long as a human's?—16 to 17 months. Or that male orcas spend their entire lives living with their mothers?

Find out from the museum how to adopt an orca. If you do adopt one, you'll get a certificate! The program helps fund orca

WHALE-WATCHING TIPS

The Whale Museum has this advice for getting the most out of your whale-watching:

- Whether you are in a boat or swimming in the water, stay 100 yards away to avoid disturbing them.

- In a boat, approach whales slowly from the side, traveling parallel to them at the same speed as the slowest whale.

- Watch for ripples or bubbles on the surface of the water. The bubbles come from an orca exhaling just before it surfaces.

- Report whale sightings to the Whale Museum's hot line by calling 800-562-8832.

research and efforts to protect the whales.

Head around the island to Lime Kiln Point State Park and try to spot whales swimming by. Bring a picnic lunch and lots of patience. It could be hours before you see a whale. This is also a good place to watch for gray whales as they head south in winter and return north in spring. For a closer look, take a cruise on a whale-watching boat. You'll find many to choose from in Friday Harbor.

WATCH THOSE FINS!

Say hello to Ruffles, Granny, Sparky, Rascal, Dylan, and their families. The orca whales living in the waters of Puget Sound have been given names. Each whale can be identified by the shape and size of its dorsal fin and by its saddle patch, the black-and-white pattern beneath and behind the fin. These are probably the most-watched whales anywhere.

Whales live in family groups called "pods." The pods always travel together. Puget Sound is home to 3 pods, with a total of more than 90 orcas. In addition to a name and number, each animal has been assigned an official letter—J, K, or L—which stands for its pod.

The whale-watching is just as good from Orcas Island. Despite all the orcas swimming around, the island was not named for whales but for a Spanish explorer. Kids like to climb to the top of Mount Constitution in Moran State Park. It is the highest point in all the San Juan Islands, and the view is great! There is camping here, too, and swimming in Cascade Lake. Care to pedal around in a paddleboat?

Eastsound, the tiny town in the middle of Orcas Island, is a good place to shop for souvenirs. Spend the afternoon in a kayak exploring the shoreline. You may see seals. Watch for deer. They swim from island to island.

If you like to bicycle, you'll want to visit Lopez Island. It's just 5 miles wide, and there aren't as many hills as on the other islands. Stop at the Spencer Spit if you like driftwood. And be sure to wave at everyone you see. It's an old Lopez custom.

Shaw Island is the smallest island served by the ferries. Franciscan nuns, wearing their traditional habits, run the ferry dock.

Fewer than 200 people live on Shaw Island. Visit the Little Red Schoolhouse. It has just 1 room, and all the island kids go to school here through 8th grade. Are your pencils sharpened? Aren't you glad you're not in school today?

KIDS! TELL YOUR PARENTS:

Camping can be a great way for a busy family to spend some time together. However, it takes planning to create a good camping experience. Everyone should pitch in! Bring along some games and tell stories around the camp fire. Don't forget the first aid kit.

For information about the San Juan Islands, call the San Juan Islands Visitors Service at 206-468-3663. Plan ahead, especially in the summer, when hotels and ferries are often crowded. Washington State Ferries can be reached at 206-464-6400. Call the Whale Museum at 206-378-4710, and the San Juan Island National Historic Park at 206-378-2240.

Many companies offer whale-watching and kayaking trips. For kayaking, try Shearwater Sea Kayak Tours at 206-376-4699. For whale-watching, call San Juan Boat Rentals and Tours at 206-378-3499.

Draw a picture of a pod of orca whales, and write a story about them. Or write about what it was like to watch for whales. Did you see any?

ollow the Canada geese.

The white-faced birds will lead you straight to Stanley Park, right in the middle of Vancouver. Nearly 1,000 of them make their home in this huge park.

Did you realize you're in a foreign country? Canadians may

look like Americans and speak the same language, but they're citizens of another nation. That's why when you crossed the border, customs officials asked your parents a few questions and might have wanted to see their proof of citizenship. There are many differences between Canada and the United States. For instance, there is a prime minister instead of a president. There is a House of Commons, not a House of Representatives. There *is* a Senate, like in the United States, but Canadian senators represent provinces instead of states. Vancouver is a city in the province of British Columbia, and its capital is Victoria. But no matter where you go, you'll find kids here that love to do the same things as you. Have you figured out Canadian money yet?

Stanley Park is the place kids love best in Vancouver. You'll see them everywhere, splashing in the water along the Seawall in

FACT:

Vancouver's Chinatown is one of the largest in the world and has been a fixture of the city since the gold rush days, more than a century ago. The Sam Kee Building in Chinatown is the world's skinniest building, just 6 feet wide.

TEA WITH AN EMPRESS

You'd better be hungry. There's tea and sandwiches and fruit and cream pastries piled high on 3-tiered plates. This isn't the place to eat and run.

Tea at Victoria's Empress Hotel is a fancy affair. If you're wearing jeans and sneakers, they won't let you in! Have you ever had milk in your tea?

When you're stuffed, walk across the street to the Royal British Columbia Museum. See the display of totem poles in Thunderbird Park. Visit a re-creation of a turn-of-the-century street, and check out the Modern History Gallery to learn about the lives of early Canadian settlers. Understand how the coastal environment has changed from the ice age to the present. Trace the history and traditions of the First Peoples. Then, learn about Canada's government at the Parliament Building nearby.

Do you like flowers? You'll probably never see as many different varieties as you will at Butchart Gardens, just outside Victoria. In the summer, come at night for the display of twinkling lights and fireworks.

Take a break and listen to the musicians playing on the Lower Causeway next to the harbor. Got a favorite tune?

summer, riding bikes, skateboarding, staring up at the giant totem poles, and watching the belugas and killer whales at the Vancouver Aquarium. And parents have just as much fun.

There's so much to do here you won't know where to start.

Take a ride on the Stanley Park Miniature Railway. Watch the graceful trumpeter swans in the Lost Lagoon. Play miniature golf. Watch a cricket match. Do you think cricket is as much fun as baseball? Rent a bike near the park entrance at Georgia Street and ride along the Seawall. It stretches for miles. But make sure to stay on the right side of the path: the other side is reserved for pedestrians.

Look for the bronze statue of the *Girl in the Wetsuit* nailed to a rock in the water. She's a famous Vancouver landmark.

In the summer, dive into the saltwater pool at Second Beach or splash and slide at the Variety Kids Water Park. There's even a gigantic blow-dryer designed for kids!

Vancouver kids also like the giant water slides at Splashdown Park, about a half hour from downtown.

For a different take on the water, visit the Vancouver Maritime Museum to see old ships and find out about the

FACT:

Beluga whales live only in arctic and subarctic areas. There are more belugas in Canada than any other kind of whale. More than 600 orcas, or killer whales, also live in British Columbia's coastal waters.

men who sailed them.

Did you see the 9 O'Clock Gun at the water's edge in Stanley Park? Originally it was fired to help ships set their clocks. Now, the old cannon is fired every night at 9 P.M. You'll hear its rumble across the city.

To find out more about Vancouver's olden days, head to the Gastown neighborhood, where the city was first settled. Did you see the steam clock?

Ready to see some whales? They live in Stanley Park—in the Vancouver Aquarium, which is famous around the world for its whale research. You can adopt an orca (also called a killer whale) here, just as you can at the Whale Museum on San Juan Island, to help support the scientists' work.

Watch the orcas at feeding time, or stare into the eyes of a giant white beluga. Some people believe that these magnificent animals belong in the wild. But scientists at the aquarium say that having them here allows you the rare chance to see whales close-up while they study them.

There are thousands of other creatures to see, too: giant fish from the Amazon Rain Forest, brilliantly colored tropical fish, sea otters, and even a giant Pacific octopus.

Outside, near Brockton Point, look for the carvings of killer whales on the giant totem poles. Two were actually "house poles" that were used inside a home to help support the beams. The grizzly bears represent power on land; the killer whales rule the sea. Many of the totem poles you'll see will have thunderbirds on top. These powerful birds played an important role in the

mythology of the First Peoples.

To see totem poles and dugout canoes and learn a lot about the First Peoples of the Northwest coast, visit the University of British Columbia's Museum of Anthropology. Check out the traditional Haida longhouse. You may meet a carver working on a totem pole.

You also could watch someone carving a cedar log into a totem pole at the Capilano Suspension Bridge and Park in north Vancouver. But first you'll want to run across the swaying bridge, 230 feet above the Capilano River. At 450 feet long, this is the longest and highest footbridge in the world— and is better than an amusement park ride! Once you've reached the other side, take a hike in Nature Park.

Just north of the bridge is the Capilano Salmon Hatchery, where 3 million eggs are hatched each year. Watch the salmon swim.

Head up the road to Grouse Mountain, where Vancouver families come to ski in the winter. Ride the gondola up to the top at night to see the city lights.

Is it time to shop until you drop? Vancouver has the perfect spot. Granville Island has a Kids Only Market full of toys, games, puzzles, books, and T-shirts just for kids. Before you leave, stop at the Public Market for a snack. There you'll find all kinds of produce from local farmers. Have a cookie from a local baker. Then head over to Science World for some experimenting. There are more than 50 hands-on exhibits here. Make music on a synthesizer or walk into a beaver lodge. Stand inside a giant camera.

Create a cyclone. You won't even have to clean it up!

KIDS! TELL YOUR PARENTS:

No matter how many great things there are to see on vacation, you'll still want to spend lots of time playing. Remember, vacations are for fun! For every indoor activity, schedule some time outdoors in a park or at the beach. Adults and kids can take turns choosing places to go. Everyone will be happier. Both Vancouver and Victoria have plenty to offer the whole family.

Ferries provide a fun and easy way to travel between Washington State and Victoria and Vancouver. It's possible to make reservations on some routes between Anacortes and Sidney, British Columbia (near Victoria). Call the Washington State Ferries at 206-464-6400 and B.C. Ferry Service at 604-669-1211. For information from Discover British Columbia, call 800-663-6000.

For a Victoria vacation planner, call 604-382-2127. To reserve tea at the Empress Hotel, call 604-384-8111.

How many differences can you list between Canada and the United States? What seems the same?

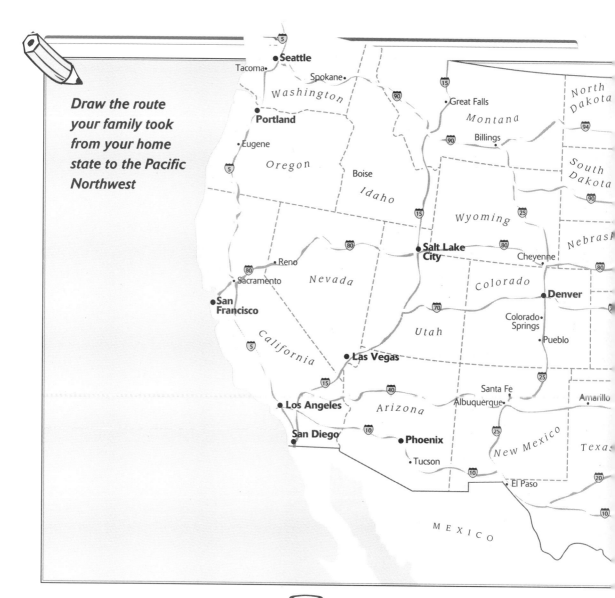

Draw the route your family took from your home state to the Pacific Northwest

Seattle
Tacoma
Spokane
Washington
Portland
Eugene
Oregon
Boise
Idaho
Great Falls
Montana
Billings
North Dakota
South Dakota
Wyoming
Cheyenne
Nebraska
Reno
Sacramento
Nevada
Salt Lake City
Colorado
Denver
San Francisco
Colorado Springs
Pueblo
Utah
California
Las Vegas
Los Angeles
Arizona
Santa Fe
Albuquerque
Amarillo
San Diego
Phoenix
New Mexico
Texas
Tucson
El Paso
MEXICO

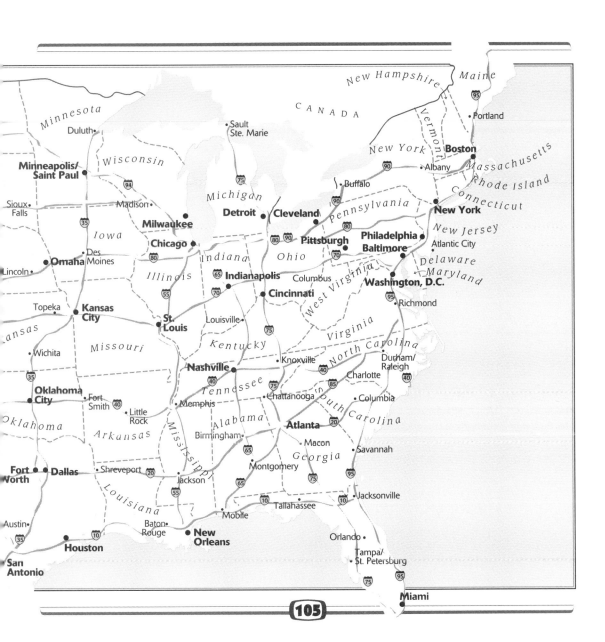

Do you want to send postcards to your friends and family at home? Write their addresses here. There's room for the addresses of the new friends you make on your trip, too!

ANSWERS TO PUZZLES

MAKE-A-WORD (page 18)

MISSOURI
OREGON
COLUMBIA
RIVER
DALLES
PIONEER
WAGON
MOUNT HOOD
BAKER CITY
TRAIL

CROSSWORD PUZZLE (page 54)

HIDDEN WORDS (page 37)

WORD JUMBLE (page 64)

APPLE
HALIBUT
HONEY STICK
CHERRIES
SHRIMP
FLOWERS
GARLIC
PEACH
JELLYBEANS
ALMONDS
CRAB
APRICOT
COOKIES
JELLY
HAZELNUT

HEY, KIDS!

What's the funniest thing that happened to your family on your trip to the Pacific Northwest? What can parents do to make family trips more fun?

Write to:

Taking the Kids

2859 Central Street, Box 119

Evanston, IL 60201

The best story may be printed in Eileen's "Taking the Kids" column in a newspaper near you!